Choosing a Pet

A Guide for Kids & the Grown-Ups Who Love Them

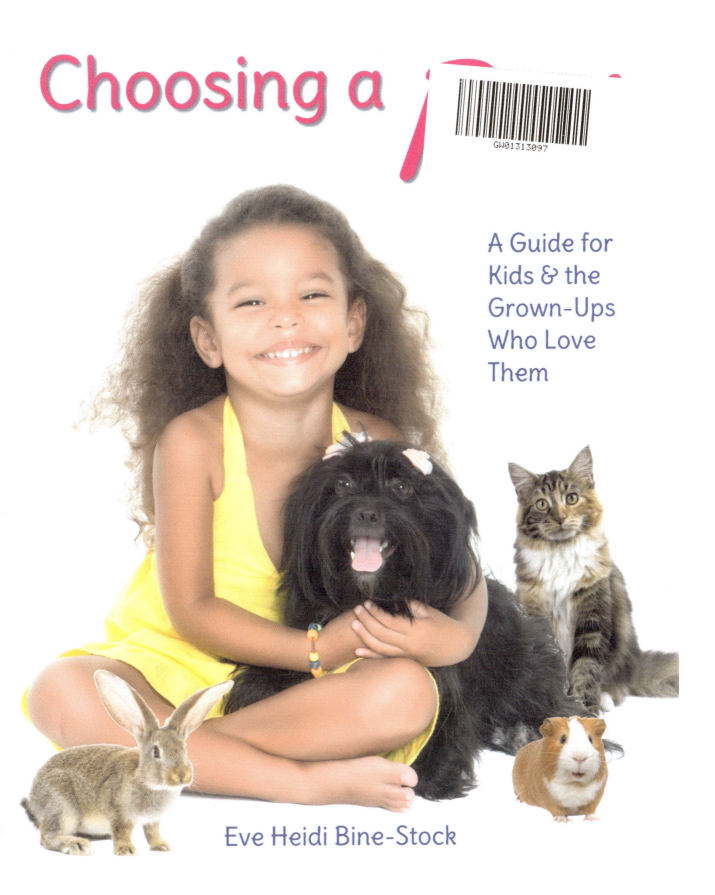

Eve Heidi Bine-Stock

CONTENTS

Introduction...............5

Dogs....................11

Cats....................17

Rabbits.................23

Guinea Pigs............29

Hamsters...............35

Congratulations........39

INTRODUCTION

Benefits of a Pet

Pets give us unconditional love. They're always happy to see us!

We can tell a pet our troubles, and it will never judge us.

Living with a pet makes us more compassionate people.

A New Family Member

A pet becomes a member of your family. We love it like family.

Since you're still young, your parent(s) must agree to adopt this new family member.

Before welcoming a pet into your family, you must commit to take care of it for its entire life. For a dog, that could mean 14 to 16 years!

What does it mean to "take care of" a pet?

Taking care of a pet means:

Feeding it

Exercising it

Training it

Grooming it

Playing with it

Cleaning up after it.

That's a lot of responsibility! Are you ready to take it on?

Plan Ahead

When choosing a pet, keep these points in mind:

- Don't mix predator and prey; snakes and cats will eat a hamster or rabbit. Cats will also eat a bird or goldfish.

- Before taking a pet home, wait until it is old enough to leave the care of its mother.

- Make sure you have the food, water, bedding, and everything else you need to take care of your new pet. You'll learn more about this in the following pages.

- Bring your new pet home at the beginning of a weekend or vacation. This way, you'll have time to get to know each other before you must return to your regular schedule.

Things to Look For

No matter what type of pet you wind up choosing, look for the marks of a healthy animal:

- ✓ Clear, bright eyes

- ✓ Clean nose, eyes and ears
    - o (not runny or crusty or oozing)

- ✓ Good covering of hair, scales, or feathers
    - o (no bald spots)

- ✓ Breathes easily
    - o (no wheeze or rattle)

- ✓ Lively and active

- ✓ Good appetite

Check the other animals in the same shelter, too—not just the one you're thinking of taking home. They should look healthy, as well. Look for clean, uncrowded cages or other living quarters; clean water; and fresh food.

Dogs

Caring for a Dog

Of all the pets in this book, a dog requires the most time, attention and effort.

A dog should be fed 2-3 times a day, at the same times each day. Always keep a bowl of fresh water available.

A dog needs to be walked 2-3 times a day, at the same times each day, in order to go to the bathroom, and to get exercise.

After a dog poops, you need to pick up the poop—with your hand inside a plastic bag, so you don't get dirty—and then throw the bag in the garbage.

You must also invest time in training your dog. Just how much time depends on what you want to teach it, and how smart the dog is.

And then there's grooming. Depending on the dog's coat, it could need grooming once a day, or once a week.

And don't forget baths! You can either do it yourself, or take your canine family member to a professional groomer. The professional can also cut the nails on the dog's paws.

A dog needs regular visits to the veterinarian, for medicine that prevents disease.

Knowing all this, if you still want a dog, read on!

Choosing the Right Dog

Choosing the "right dog" means, first of all, knowing yourself. After all, you are one-half of the relationship. So before you begin searching for a dog, answer these questions about yourself:

- ✓ **Are you new to dogs?** Have a dog now? Had one in the past?

- ✓ **What type of home** do you live in? Apartment? House with yard?

- ✓ **What size of dog** do you want?

- ✓ **How much time** do you have available to exercise, train, and groom a dog?

- ✓ How active are you?

- ✓ What do you want to do with your dog? Cuddle, mostly? Play a lot? Run?

- ✓ What is your tolerance for barking, shedding and drooling?

- ✓ Is anyone in your family allergic to dogs?

Several sites online have quizzes to help you find the right dog match. Here are two recommended sites:

Pure-bred matches only:
https://www.pedigree.com/getting-a-new-dog/breed-match

Both pure-bred and mixed-breed matches:
https://dogtime.com/quiz/dog-breed-selector

Where to Get a Dog

Animal shelters, humane societies, and breed rescue groups specialize in finding new homes for dogs whose first homes did not work out, usually due to the ignorance of the pet parent.

Animal shelters and humane societies house many dogs of different kinds and ages, both pure-bred and mixed-breed.

Breed rescue groups temporarily place a pure-bred or mixed-breed dog with a foster family, until it is adopted by a forever home. You usually don't have numerous dogs to choose from.

Animal shelters, humane societies, and breed rescue groups charge low fees, and have already spayed or neutered the dogs. This makes the dogs happier and healthier, and prevents unwanted litters.

Breeders specialize in pure-bred dogs, and usually find homes for puppies. You can find a good breeder by asking for referrals from dog trainers, kennel clubs, and veterinarians. Breeders don't typically spay or neuter their dogs.

Prepare for Your Dog

Be sure that you have these items for your new dog:

- Leash
- Collar
- ID tag
- Dog food
- Food dish
- Water dish
- Crate or pen with bed
- Chew toys
- Play toys
- Grooming brush
- Nail trimmer
- Flea control products
- Dog license
- Book on dog care and training

CATS

Caring for a Cat

Cats are relatively easy to care for. They don't require much time or work, but need exercise through play at least twice a day for 15-20 minutes each session.

Cats sleep an average of 16 hours a day, and spend up to half their waking hours in grooming themselves.

Kittens should be fed 2-3 times a day. Grown-up cats (one year old and up) should be fed once or twice a day. Always keep a bowl of clean water available.

Cats keep themselves very clean. They constantly groom themselves with their tongue. Rarely do they need a bath. But you must brush them regularly, to reduce shedding, and the number of hairballs they might spit up.

Keep a litter box for your cat to go to the bathroom, and clean out the poop every day with a slotted litter scoop. A cat won't use a dirty litter box, so at least once a week, throw out the used kitty litter, wash the box, and fill the box with fresh litter.

Have a stable, sturdy scratching post for your cat to use. And trim your cat's nails every two weeks.Doing both will cut down on scratched arms and furniture.

Keep your cat indoors. Cats that go outdoors get fleas, and can be hurt by vehicles, and by other animals. Place a collar and ID tag on your cat, in case it sneaks outdoors and gets lost.

A cat needs yearly visits to the veterinarian, for check-ups, and medicine to prevent disease.

Choosing the Purr-fect Cat

Don't choose a cat based on looks alone, or take the first cat you like. You might think that you want a long-hair cat, but find yourself drawn to a short-hair cat in the last cage at the shelter. When you feel a special connection with a particular cat, that one is your best bet.

The American Veterinary Medical Association gives good advice for choosing a cat: Pick one that is active, inquisitive, and seeks affection and attention from people. An adult cat should allow handling and petting without hissing or scratching. A kitten should be relaxed when picked up and handled. The best age at which to obtain a kitten is when it is between 7 and 9 weeks old.

Where to Get a Cat

Animal shelters, humane societies, and breed rescue groups specialize in finding new homes for cats whose first homes did not work out, usually due to the ignorance of the pet parent.

Animal shelters and humane societies house many cats of different kinds and ages, both pure-bred and mixed-breed.

Breed rescue groups temporarily place a pure-bred or mixed-breed cat with a foster family, until it is adopted by a forever home.

Animal shelters, humane societies, and breed rescue groups charge low fees, and have already spayed or neutered the cats. This makes the cats happier and healthier, and prevents unwanted litters.

Breeders specialize in pure-bred cats, both adults and kittens. You can find a good breeder by asking for referrals from a veterinarian. Breeders don't typically spay or neuter their cats.

Prepare for Your Cat

Be sure that you have these items for your new cat or kitten:

- Cat carrier
- Collar
- ID tag
- Cat food
- Food dish
- Water dish
- Bed
- Play toys
- Scratching post
- Grooming brush
- Nail trimmer
- Cat litter box and litter scoop
- Cat litter
- Book on cat care and behavior

RABBITS

Caring for a Rabbit

Rabbits require less time and attention than dogs, but more than cats.

To keep your bunny happy, spend 1-2 hours a day playing with and petting it.

Let your rabbit out of its cage to roam inside your home—or just one room like the kitchen—for 1-4 hours a day. Keep a close eye on it, so it doesn't get into mischief. Never leave your rabbit in its cage for a whole 24 hours at a time.

Rabbits should be fed twice a day. They eat mostly hay, and fresh veggies such as carrot tops. Rabbits always need fresh water available.

Rabbits eat their first, soft poop because they need to digest everything twice to get enough nutrients. The second poop comes out as small, hard pellets which rabbits don't eat. (If this sounds gross, maybe a rabbit is not the right pet for you.)

Rabbits poop often because they constantly nibble hay. Your rabbit can be trained to use a litter box kept in its cage. You'll need to clean out the dry poop at least once a day with a slotted litter scoop.

Rabbits like to chew and scratch because their teeth and claws never stop growing. Give your rabbit chew toys, and trim its claws about once a month.

Rabbits clean themselves; don't bathe them; it can make them sick.

You need to take your bunny to a veterinarian for "exotic" pets; most "dog and cat vets" can't care for rabbits.

Choosing the Right Rabbit

While there are dozens of breeds, these in particular—Dutch, mini Rex, Lionhead, and Lops—are bred to be calm and friendly, and make a good addition to a family. These breeds are small, so they are easier to handle, and need less cage space, than bigger rabbits.

The American Veterinary Medical Association says to choose a bunny that is alert and active. It should be plump and well-fed, with shiny, lush fur. Make sure that it has been handled by humans, so it is comfortable with people, and will make a good pet.

Where to Get a Rabbit

Animal shelters, humane societies, and breed rescue groups specialize in finding new homes for rabbits whose first homes did not work out, usually due to the ignorance of the pet parent.

Animal shelters and humane societies house rabbits of different kinds and ages, both pure-bred and mixed-breed.

Breed rescue groups temporarily place a pure-bred or mixed-breed rabbit with a foster family, until it is adopted by a forever home.

Animal shelters, humane societies, and breed rescue groups charge low fees, and have already spayed or neutered the rabbits. This makes the rabbits happier and healthier, and prevents unwanted litters.

Breeders specialize in pure-bred cats, both adults and kits. You can find a good breeder by asking for referrals from a veterinarian. Breeders don't typically spay or neuter their rabbits.

Prepare for Your Rabbit

Be sure that you have these items for your new rabbit:

- Rabbit carrier
- Rabbit cage
- Hay rack
- Bedding material
- Hideaway
- Food dish
- Rabbit food pellets & fresh greens
- Water bowl and water bottle
- Chewing blocks
- Play toys
- Harness and leash
- Grooming brush
- Nail trimmer
- Litter box and litter scoop
- Book on rabbit care and behavior

Guinea Pigs

Caring for a Guinea Pig

Guinea pigs (also called cavies) are social animals. To keep one happy, be sure to play with it, cuddle it, and pet it frequently.

Keep your guinea pig's cage away from drafts and direct sunlight, but in an area the family uses regularly.

A guinea pig needs daily exercise, so let it scurry for an hour around a room—like the kitchen—that has a pet-proof floor.

A guinea pig can be trained to use a litter box.

Spot-clean inside the cage and litter box every day, and freshen the cage weekly from top to bottom.

Feed your guinea pig twice a day, morning and evening. It needs pellets specially made for guinea pigs, as well as a constant supply of grass hay, and fresh water. Feed it fresh veggies like cabbage, carrots, and broccoli. Give it vitamin C, too; it needs this to stay healthy.

Provide chew toys for your guinea pig. It likes to chew because its teeth grow continually. Trim its claws once a month.

Your guinea pig needs a veterinarian who specializes in "exotic pets" or "small pets."

Choosing the Right Guinea Pig

There are dozens of different breeds available: short hair, long hair; smooth, fuzzy, curly hair; in a range of colors and color combinations.

Unlike dogs, there's not much difference in temperament or instinct among guinea pig breeds. So just choose a healthy one whose looks appeal to you, and whose hair you have time to groom.

Your guinea pig may be shy at first; give it time to warm up to you.

Where to Get a Guinea Pig

Animal shelters, humane societies, and breed rescue groups specialize in finding new homes for guinea pigs whose first homes did not work out, usually due to the ignorance of the pet parent.

Animal shelters and humane societies house guinea pigs of different kinds and ages, both pure-bred and mixed-breed, and charge low fees.

Breed rescue groups temporarily place a pure-bred or mixed-breed guinea pig with a foster family, until it is adopted by a forever home.

Breeders specialize in pure-bred guinea pigs. A "small pets" veterinarian can refer you to a reputable breeder.

Prepare for Your Guinea Pig

Be sure that you have these items for your new guinea pig:

- Pet carrier
- Guinea pig cage
- Hay rack
- Bedding material
- Hideaway
- Food dish
- Guinea pig food pellets & fresh veggies
- Water bowl and water bottle
- Chewing blocks
- Play toys
- Grooming brush
- Nail trimmer
- Litter box and litter scoop
- Book on guinea pig care and behavior

HAMSTERS

Caring for a Hamster

Keep your hamster's habitat in a quiet, low-traffic area of your home, away from drafts and direct sunlight.

A hamster likes to live alone, not with other hamsters.

Allow your hamster to gradually get used to you until you can hold it in your hands. This process may take weeks.

Hamsters are nocturnal (active at night). Never wake up your hamster; it will be startled and probably bite you. Play with your hamster every evening, when it's awake.

A hamster needs a lot of exercise. It enjoys running around and around on a hamster wheel inside its habitat. You can also put your hamster into a hollow, plastic exercise ball, to roll along the floor.

A hamster likes to burrow, so provide deep bedding in its habitat. It also hordes food, so every day look for, and replace, hidden stashes of food.

Hamsters also like to gnaw and chew, so give yours chew toys; this will keep its ever-growing teeth from getting too long.

Feed your hamster food pellets (so it can't pick out its favorite ingredients). Supplement your hamster's diet with leafy, dark green vegetables, and bits of fruit such as apple, banana, or melon. A raisin makes a good treat.

Always keep a bottle of fresh water available.

A hamster can be trained to use a litter box. Clean the litter box every day, and freshen the entire habitat and its contents once a week.

Your hamster needs a veterinarian who specializes in "exotic pets" or "small pets."

Choosing the Right Hamster

While there are several breeds available, your best bet is the friendly, easy-to-handle Syrian hamster (also known as the Golden, or the Teddy Bear).

The Syrian breed comes in different colors and coat lengths, so choose one whose looks you fancy.

The male Syrian hamster is more calm and friendly than the female, and also smells better. Best advice? Stick with a male Syrian.

Where to Get a Hamster

It's recommended to adopt a Syrian hamster from an animal shelter, humane society, or small-animal breed rescue group. They truly care about your pet's welfare.

Prepare for Your Hamster

Be sure that you have these items for your new hamster:

- Small holding cage
- Hamster habitat
- Bedding material
- Hideaway
- Food dish
- Hamster food pellets & fresh veggies
- Water bottle
- Chewing blocks
- Exercise toys
- Climbing toys
- Grooming brush
- Litter box and litter scoop
- Book on hamster care and behavior

CONGRATULATIONS

Whichever pet you take home with you, be sure to treat it gently, so you don't frighten or harm it.

Best wishes for a long, loving relationship with your new family member!

Copyright © 2021 Eve Heidi Bine-Stock

ISBN-13: 9798465367677

All rights reserved. This book may not be reproduced
in whole or in part in any form, or by any means,
without express written permission from the author.

Contact the Author:
Eve Heidi Bine-Stock
P.O. Box 3346
Omaha, NE 68103
EveHeidiWrites@gmail.com

Thank you to
my mother, Shirley Smalheiser,
and my friend, Ralph Rahn, Jr.,
for their love, encouragement, and feedback.

Photographs sourced from Adobe Stock.

Printed in Great Britain
by Amazon